In Two Worlds

Chapters

by Michael Burgan
illustrated by Oki Han

**Harcourt**

Orlando Boston Dallas Chicago San Diego

Visit *The Learning Site!*

www.harcourtschool.com

A Writer's Life

For many years, Bette Bao Lord has been a popular writer, and her books are read around the world. Bette says writing is not always easy. It may take her twenty tries to get one chapter just right. Her readers, however, are glad she so stubbornly looks for the perfect word.

Bette did not plan to become a writer. In college, she studied history. She also learned about diplomacy, or how nations deal with each other. Later, however, Bette saw she had many special stories she could tell.

Bette Bao was born on November 3, 1938, in Shanghai, China. Her mother named her after Bette Davis, a famous American movie star. Bette Bao's father was an engineer. He had studied in England and spoke excellent English.

When Bette was born, Mr. Bao was working for the Chinese government. This was a difficult time for the Chinese, since their country was at war with Japan. Bombs often exploded around the Baos' home.

The war against Japan ended in 1945, and Mr. Bao continued to work for the government. The next year, he went to the United States to buy machines for his homeland. He had to leave his family behind, but soon he made plans to have them join him in America. There was a problem, though. Only Mrs. Bao, Bette, and another daughter could come. Bette's youngest sister, Sansan, had to stay in China with relatives.

Bette's Long Journey

Trying to Fit In

Bette and her family settled in Brooklyn, New York. Bette was put in the fifth grade, even though she was only eight years old. She did not speak English, and she was the only Chinese student in her class. Her parents told her not to grumble about how hard it was to fit into her new home. They expected Bette to be bright and well behaved. Even if she did not understand everything her teacher said, she should do her best to learn.

Over time, the Baos decided not to go back to China. Bette realized she would be living in the United States for a long time. She learned English, studied hard, and made friends. After college, she went to a school to learn about law and diplomacy. There she met a young man named Winston Lord. He was studying to become a diplomat. In 1963, they were married.

Their backgrounds were very different. Love and acceptance from both families helped Bette and Winston begin their life together.

Seventeen years after the family had left China, Mrs. Bao arranged for Sansan, Bette's youngest sister, to meet her in the city of Hong Kong. When they saw each other, Sansan darted over like a streak. Sansan then came with Mrs. Bao to New York. This was the year before Bette's wedding. Bette finally got to see Sansan for the first time in seventeen years.

When Bette left China, Sansan was a baby; now she was a teenager. Bette and Sansan spent many hours talking about China. Bette wrote about her sister in her first book, *Eighth Moon*.

Eighth Moon quickly became a success. Bette, however did not continue writing. Instead, she taught modern dance in Washington, D.C., where she and Winston were raising a family. Winston was now a successful diplomat. His most important job came in 1971, when he helped the United States and China form ties with each other for the first time in more than twenty years. Two years later, Winston traveled to China. Bette went with him.

The trip was exciting for Bette, for she visited relatives she had not seen since 1946. The trip also connected Bette to the Chinese side of her life. She had been in America for so long that she had forgotten how to speak Chinese. She had to learn it all over again.

Bette had lived in two different countries and now spoke two languages. When she returned to America, Bette decided to write a book about China. She wanted to tell Americans about her homeland and its people.

This new book was hard to write. Bette spent six years working on it, writing mostly late at night. In the end, however, she produced a great book called *Spring Moon* that was sold around the world. People enjoyed this story of a Chinese family dealing with the changes going on in their country. The main character is a woman named Spring Moon. Bette was often asked to speak about the book and her experiences as a Chinese American.

Spring Moon was published in 1981. A few years later, Bette wrote her third book. To many readers, this is her best one. Bette decided to write about her own experiences as a young Chinese girl coming to America. She called the book *In the Year of the Boar and Jackie Robinson*. The book is set in 1947, the year Bette started grade school. The story is about a young girl named Shirley Temple Wong who is the only Chinese student in her class.

Shirley, Mabel, and Jackie

In the Year of the Boar and Jackie Robinson is fiction. Shirley, however, is based on Bette. Both of them were named after movie stars. Shirley faces many of the problems Bette had as a child. For example, Shirley has trouble speaking English. When the class says the Pledge of Allegiance, the other students mumbled, so Shirley doesn't learn it correctly. When she says it, it comes out "I pledge a lesson to the frog." Shirley also has a hard time getting along with some of her classmates.

Shirley tries to play stickball. This game is like baseball and is often played in city streets. The cries of the players mix with the screech of tires from nearby cars.

At first Shirley is not very good at stickball. The other kids don't want her to play. Then she becomes friends with Mabel, the biggest and strongest girl in the fifth grade. Mabel picks Shirley for her team, and Shirley begins to play better.

Shirley also becomes a huge fan of the Brooklyn Dodgers. The year 1947 was special for that baseball team. One of their best players was Jackie Robinson—the first African American to play in the Major Leagues. Jackie is Shirley's hero. At the end of the book, she meets Jackie. For Shirley, baseball helps make her feel at home in America. Bette said that she wrote this book to show that Chinese Americans can choose the best of their new home and their old.

Soon after she wrote *In the Year of the Boar and Jackie Robinson*, Bette returned to China. This trip, however, was not just a visit. In 1985, Winston became ambassador to China. In that role, he looked out for the interests of the United States in China. Bette and Winston stayed in China for almost four years. When she returned to the United States, Bette wrote a book called *Legacies* about the Chinese people she knew and how they lived.

Bette wrote another book about China called *The Middle Heart*. The book is fiction and describes life in China during most of the twentieth century.

Today Bette remains active as a public speaker. She also works with Freedom House, a group that tries to spread democracy around the world. Still, Bette is best known for her books, which have helped Americans understand China and the Chinese people. As a writer, Bette has found a way to bring together her two worlds.